THE Journey

REFLECTIONS — for the — time of

Grieving

JOHN L. BELL

INCLUDING A CD OF 17 SONGS

spck

Originally published in the United States of America in 1996
by GIA Publications, Inc., Chicago, Illinois

First published in Great Britain in 2018

Society for Promoting Christian Knowledge
36 Causton Street
London SW1P 4ST
www.spck.org.uk

British Library Cataloguing-in-Publication Data
A catalogue record for this book is available from the British Library

ISBN 978–0–281–08002–1

Designed and typeset by Fiona Andreanelli
First printed in Great Britain by Jellyfish Print Solutions
Subsequently digitally printed in Great Britain

Produced on paper from sustainable forests

Contents

Using the Recording

While most collections of songs are intended to be listened to from start to finish, the nature of this material may suggest alternative uses.

The songs are arranged in broad categories that roughly represent different stages of the grieving process. If the listener is going through a bereavement, it may therefore be best to listen only to one section at a time.

Again, some of these songs are of a highly individual nature, while others are meant for corporate use. Depending on the circumstances, personal songs may be more important for people who are grieving than public ones.

However, it is hoped that the full spectrum of text and emotion will eventually be listened to or used by everyone, because grief is a process, not a destination. Feeling lost, being puzzled, letting go and gladly remembering are part of a continuum, and our spiritual health requires that we go through it, rather than remain numb with no desire to recover, or sing victorious hallelujahs to avoid dealing with the mess inside.

The text of the songs is given, along with a note on each item and some words of Scripture and prayer that may be helpful in times of sorrow.

Introduction

These songs started many years ago. Exactly how many, we don't know, but the need to express grief, to sing our sorrow, is as old as humanity.

When it came to collecting together the items that would eventually make what we call the book of Psalms, the selectors were careful to ensure that the texts would be fully representative of the providence of God and the experience of humanity.

That is why side by side with expressions of deepest praise are cries of unfathomable despair. Both are not only acceptable to God, they are essential for our mental and spiritual health.

So it is that today when we walk in darkness, or wonder at the injustice of accidental death, or are pained by the sight of people we love withering away, we find an uncanny resonance in such words as, 'How long, O Lord, will you forget me?'

The words, written under different skies and in a different age, articulate across the centuries the things we want to say, giving us permission to question, to rage and to doubt; and offering us the ultimate consolation when we realize that all such expressions were used by Jesus, who, as a first-century rabbi, loved the psalms and knew them all by heart.

This collection does not simply consist of psalms of lament. It contains three spirituals, two of which are well known yet deserve to be revisited, because the spirituals were often born in places where people were compelled to demand that the doors of heaven be open in the face of the jaws of hell. They convey, through abject simplicity of language, a tough faith and a tested hope.

But there also songs that were written after hearing the testimony of the pain of particular individuals, and one in response to a nation's pain. It happened when an unspeakable sense of tragedy overwhelmed the people of Scotland as the news broke of the killing of sixteen young children and their school teacher in the cathedral town of Dunblane.

People there had hitherto lived quiet lives in a quiet place, renowned to some for its medieval architecture, to others as one of the birthing rooms of the 1960s hymn explosion, and to others as a centre of ecumenical cooperation. Suddenly it and its citizens became headline news across the world, and parents everywhere clasped their children closer while feeling for those in Dunblane whose arms were empty and whose grief was raw.

This collection and its accompanying CD were originally suggested by our North American publisher, GIA of Chicago. With a generosity of spirit rare in the publishing world, they were not seeking a 'bestseller' but rather a pastoral resource for public and private use. Over the intervening years, The Last Journey has proven its worth in times of corporate grief, such as those following school shootings, and for bereft individuals who need to know that they do not grieve alone. Others have been there before, and God inhabits their pain.

My colleagues and I are deeply appreciative of the invitation by SPCK to make the songs available in the UK.

JOHN L. BELL, Easter 2018

I. IN THE BEGINNING

when Jesus saw Mary weeping and the people who had come with her weeping, he was moved with indignation and

deeply distressed.
'Where have you
laid Lazarus?' he
asked. They replied,
'Come and see.'
Jesus wept.

John 11:33-35

Prayer

What did they think, Lord, those who watched you cry
in front of women, in front of other men,
for your dead friend, or your favourite city?

Did they admire your tenderness having seen your toughness?
Were they disgusted by your tears and loss of self-control?
Or were they drawn into your sorrow for the plight of the world
and the pain of its people?

Help me to share the solidarity of your deep sorrow
so that I can share the certainty of your deeper joy.

O Christ, you wept

Traditionally, the association of Jesus with humanity is spoken of in terms of him being 'like us in all things, yet without sin'. What is sometimes forgotten is that he also shares with us a solidarity in grief. When our hearts break for the loss of a friend, he knows what it feels like. He has been there too.

O CHRIST, YOU WEPT

WORDS: **John L. Bell and Graham Maule**
TUNE: **Palmer (JLB)**

O Christ, you wept when grief was raw,
and felt for those who mourned a friend;
come close to where we would not be
and hold us, numbed by this life's end.

The well-loved voice is silent now
and we have much we meant to say;
collect our lost and wandering words
and keep them till the endless day.

We try to hold what is not here
and fear for what we do not know.
Oh, take our hands in yours, good Lord,
and free us to let our friend go.

In all our loneliness and doubt,
beyond what we can realize,
address us from your empty tomb
and tell us that life never dies.

II. GRIEF, FEAR AND ABANDONMENT

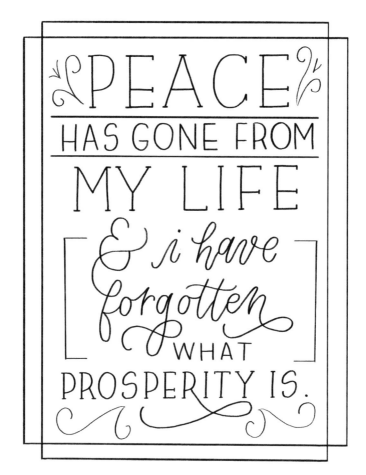

PEACE HAS GONE FROM MY LIFE & i have forgotten WHAT PROSPERITY IS.

then i
CRY OUT
—THAT MY—
Strength
HAS GONE AND
—so has my—
hope IN THE LORD.
Lamentations 3:17-18

Holy God, when a child dies in the womb
or lives only for an hour,
is this your will?

When a life full of energy
is cut down in its prime,
is this your will?

When eyes we loved don't recognize us,
and the body turns too fragile to embrace,
and hope dies before life expires,
is this your will?

I ask, Lord, because I need to ask.
And even if, on this side of time,
no answers are evident,
I want to know that you hear my prayer.

Psalm 13 begins with this brief lament, here set to a slightly bluesy tune, because **the blues find their genesis not in the music industry, but in sorrow.**

HOW LONG, O LORD?

WORDS: **Psalm 13, paraphrased JLB**
TUNE: **New 13th (JLB)**

How long, O Lord, will you quite forget me?
How long, O Lord, will you turn your face from me?
How long, O Lord, must I suffer in my soul?
How long, how long, O Lord?

How long, O Lord, must this grief possess my heart?
How long, O Lord, must I languish night and day?
How long, O Lord, shall my enemy oppress?
How long, how long, O Lord?

Look now, look now and answer me, my God;
give light, give light lest I sleep the sleep of death.
Lest my enemies rejoice at my downfall,
look now, look now, O Lord.

I cry to God

Psalm 77 provides the text for this song. It is a more complex poem than Psalm 13. It illustrates the confusion within the mind of someone who is in agony. Hearing voices is not the sole prerogative of the schizophrenic. **Anyone whose life has been torn apart by grief can be unsettled by random and conflicting thoughts which assail the mind that longs for peace.**

I CRY TO GOD

WORDS: **Psalm 77, paraphrased JLB**
TUNE: **New 77th (JLB)**

I cry to God and he hears me:
in my time of trouble I seek him.
By night my hands plead in prayer,
but I find nothing for my comfort.

I think of God and I moan;
I meditate and feel useless.
God keeps the sleep from my eyes,
and my speech is lost in confusion.

I thought of days gone by,
and remembered times now vanished.
I spent the night in deep distress
while my spirit murmured within me.

Will God reject us for ever?
Will God refuse us his mercy?
Has endless love reached an end?
Are God's promises now invalid?

Has God forgotten to be gracious?
Has anger doused his compassion?
Has God's mighty arm lost its grasp?
Does it hang powerless beside him?

Let me now remember God's work
and recall his wonderful greatness.
Let me meditate on his power
and remember all God has done.

Who is there to understand?

In the tradition of the original psalmists, this text is a transcription of someone else's experience which cried out to be expressed before God. A conversation with a friend who was counselling someone **in the throes of despair** supplied the words for the first three verses, to which **the voice of God responds in the last.**

WHO IS THERE TO UNDERSTAND?

WORDS: **John L. Bell**

TUNE: **Carrington**

All the fears I need to name but am too scared to say;
all the shame for what I've done which nothing can allay;
all the people I've let down and lost along the way;
all the hate I still remand.

> Must these torment me to the end of time?
> Who is there to understand?

All the wasted years in which I struggled to be free;
all the broken promises that took their toll on me;
all the love I should have shown and all I failed to be;
all I longed to take my hand.

> Must these torment me to the end of time?
> Who is there to understand?

What the cause of pain is and, much more, the reason why;
what my final hour will bring, how suddenly I'll die;
what the future holds for those I'll miss, for whom I cry;
what, too late, I might demand.
   Shall these torment me to the end of time?
   Who is there to understand?

'All the wrong you now admit, I promise to forgive;
all that you regret you are not sentenced to relive;
all the love you've never known is mine alone to give;
you, my child, are understood.
   So do not fear all that is yet to be:
   heaven is close and God is good.'

III. CONSOLATION

Scripture

Jesus said, 'All that the Father gives me will come to me, and anyone who comes to me I will never turn away. I have come down from heaven, to do not my own will, but the will of him who sent me. It is his will that I should not lose even one of those he has given me, but should raise them all up on the last day. For it is my Father's will that everyone who sees the Son and has faith in him should have eternal life; and I will raise them up on the last day.'

John 6.37–40

Prayer

When the hearse stops
and the mourners gather,
and the air is solemn,
and choking people whisper, 'I'm sorry . . .'
be there today, Lord.

Where the hardly worn clothes are parcelled,
and the insurances are cancelled,
and a weary voice on the telephone says,
'She's not here any more' . . .
be there today, Lord.

And where people can't cry
or won't cry
or turn, raging to heaven and ask,
'Why him? Why now?' . . .
be there today, Lord.

You won't have to do much.
Your presence will be everything.

Let your restless hearts be still

In prayer, as in worship, we are caught up in an interchange between what God has to say to us and what we need to say to God.

For centuries, 'Kyrie eleison' (Lord, have mercy) has been the petition that asks God for help. Here it provides the backcloth for the divine response – tender words of strong reassurance from St John's Gospel.

LET YOUR RESTLESS HEARTS BE STILL

WORDS: **John 14, paraphrased JLB**

TUNE: **The lark in the clear air (Irish traditional), arr. JLB**

Kyrie eleison, Kyrie eleison.
Kyrie eleison, Kyrie eleison.

Let your restless hearts be still,
let your troubled minds be rested;
trust in God to lift your care
and, in caring, trust in me.
In God's house you have a place –
were it otherwise, I would have told you:
this I gladly go to prepare
and make ready for you all.

Where I am and where I will be
is where you shall live for ever;
and the way to where I go
I have walked among you here.
I'm the Way that never ends,
I'm the Truth that never changes,
I'm the Life that never dies
but delights to love you all.

O the Lamb

A traditional North American text and tune are the basis of this choral arrangement which celebrates that the Christ who prays for us in eternity is the one who was hanged for us in time.

O THE LAMB

WORDS: **Traditional**

TUNE: **The Christian lyre, 1833, arr. JLB**

O the Lamb, the loving Lamb,
the Lamb of Calvary!
The Lamb that was slain,
yet lives again
to intercede for me.

Steal away

This African-American spiritual was a source of strength to black slaves who believed in a liberating Lord over and against the earthly masters who demanded subservience. It still yields consolation to people who feel crushed by the tragedy or pain of life. And it is not pious escapism either to want to be relieved of torment, or to proclaim that God calls to a reality that is bigger than ours.

STEAL AWAY

WORDS: **Traditional**
TUNE: **Traditional, arr. JLB**

Steal away, steal away.
Steal away to Jesus.
Steal away, steal away home;
I ain't got long to stay here.

My Lord, he calls me;
he calls me by the thunder.
The trumpet sounds within-a my soul;
I ain't got long to stay here.

Green trees are bendin',
poor sinner starts a-tremblin'.
The trumpet sounds within-a my soul;
I ain't got long to stay here.

Tombstones are burstin',
poor sinner starts a-tremblin'.
The trumpet sounds within-a my soul;
I ain't got long to stay here.

My Lord, he calls me;
he calls me by the lightnin'.
The trumpet sounds within-a my soul;
I ain't got long to stay here.

The last journey

Legend has it that the tune of this song was played when the ancient kings of Scotland were ferried from the mainland to their resting place on the island of Iona. The text indicates how, in leaving the community of God's people on earth, we do not become lonely, forgotten souls, but are companioned by the perfect community of the three-personed God and the angels of heaven.

THE LAST JOURNEY

WORDS: **John L. Bell and Graham Maule**
TUNE: **Iona boat song (Scottish traditional), arr. JLB**

From the falter of breath,
through the silence of death,
to the wonder that's breaking beyond;
God has woven a way,
unapparent by day,
for all those of whom heaven is fond.

From frustration and pain,
through hope hard to sustain,
to the wholeness here promised, there known;
Christ has gone where we fear
and has vowed to be near
on the journey we make on our own.

From the dimming of light,
through the darkness of night,
to the glory of goodness above;
God the Spirit is sent
to ensure heaven's intent
is embraced and completed in love.

From today till we die,
through all questioning why,
to the place from which time and tide flow;
angels tread on our dreams
and magnificent themes
of heaven's promise are echoed below.

IV. LEAVE TAKING

Scripture

I reckon that the sufferings we now endure bear no comparison with the glory, as yet unrevealed, which is in store for us. In everything, as we know, the Spirit co-operates for good with those who love God and are called according to his purpose. For I am convinced that there is nothing in death or life, in the realm of spirits or superhuman powers, in the world as it is or the world as it shall be, in the forces of the universe, in the heights or depths – nothing in all creation that can separate us from the love of God in Christ Jesus our Lord.

Romans 8.18, 28, 38–39

Prayer

God, help me to let go.

The last word has not been said,
the last embrace has not been given,
the last will is not final.

There will be another time,
a better place, a fonder embrace.
But that cannot happen
until I put into your hands
the one who has held on to mine.
God, help me to let go,
and then to grow.

this is a song of
corporate grief,
such as one finds
at a funeral
where very
different people,
whose lives have

been touched by a friend they had in common, feel a strange closeness to each other.

SINCE WE ARE SUMMONED

WORDS: **John L. Bell**
TUNE: **Silent place (JLB)**

Since we are summoned to a silent place,
struggling to find some words to fill the space;
Christ be beside us as we grieve,
daring to doubt or to believe.

Since we are savaged by the pain of loss,
stopped at a barrier we have yet to cross;
Christ be beside us as we mourn,
broken, disconsolate and torn.

.

Since we are forced to face this last farewell,
saddened to depths we never could foretell;
Christ be beside us as we weep,
loosening our hold on whom you'll keep.

Christ be beneath us, Christ be all above,
Christ take the hand of her we've lost and love;
take her to paradise and then
Christ be beside us once again.

go, silent friend

This song was written for the funeral of a very unassuming Dutch woman who died in Amsterdam in her nineties. It was only after her death that people became aware of how she, who had cleaned offices for most of her working life, had actually been a law-breaker. During the Second World War, when Holland was occupied, she defied Nazi authorities and risked her own life by sheltering a sophisticated Jewish refugee. Hers was a timely death, and her funeral was as full of gratitude as of grief.

GO, SILENT FRIEND

WORDS: **John L. Bell**

TUNE: **Genevan Psalm 12, arr. JLB**

Go, silent friend,
your life has found its ending;
to dust returns
your weary mortal frame.
God, who before birth
called you into being,
now calls you hence,
his accent still the same.

Go, silent friend,
your life in Christ is buried;
for you he lived
and died and rose again.
Close by his side
your promised place is waiting
where, fully known,
you shall with God remain.

Go, silent friend,
forgive us if we grieved you;
safe now in heaven,
kindly say our name.
Your life has touched us,
that is why we mourn you;
our lives without you
cannot be the same.

Go, silent friend,
we do not grudge you glory;
sing, sing with joy
deep praises to your Lord.
You, who believed that Christ
would come back for you,
now celebrate
that Jesus keeps his word.

Lord our God, receive your servant

This is a setting of the words associated with the 'Song of Farewell', the point in the Roman Catholic Requiem Mass where the congregation collectively entrust the one they mourn into the hands of the angels of God.

LORD OUR GOD, RECEIVE YOUR SERVANT

WORDS: **The Roman Missal**

TUNE: **John L. Bell**

Lord our God, receive your servant,
Lord our God, receive your servant,
for whom you shed your blood,
shed your blood.

Remember, Lord, that we are dust,
like grass, like a flower of the field.
One moment we burst into bloom,
then vanish, vanish for ever.

Saints of God, come to *her* aid,
bid *her* welcome, you angels of the Lord.
Receive, receive *her* soul
and present *her* to God the Most High.

Now let eternal rest
be granted to *her*, O Lord;
and let perpetual light
shine, shine upon *her*.

Agnus Dei

The Latin text is an ancient liturgical prayer asking for rest and perpetual light to be granted to those who have died.

AGNUS DEI

WORDS: **The Roman Missal**

TUNE: **John L. Bell**

Agnus Dei, qui tollis peccata mundi:
dona eis requiem, requiem.
Lux perpetua luceat eis,
cum sanctis tuis in aeternum,
Domine quia pius es.
Requiem aeternum
dona eis Domine,
et lux perpetua luceat eis.

Lamb of God, who takes away
the sin of the world,
give them peace.
May perpetual light shine on them
with your saints in glory, Lord,
because you are just.
Give them peace, Lord,
and let perpetual light shine on them.

V. THE SAINTS IN HEAVEN

Scripture

I saw a new heaven and a new earth, for the first heaven and the first earth had vanished, and there was no longer any sea. I saw the Holy City, new Jerusalem, coming down out of heaven from God, made ready like a bride adorned for her husband. I heard a loud voice proclaiming from the throne: 'Now God has his dwelling with humankind! God will dwell among them and they shall be his people, and God himself will be with them. He will wipe every tear from their eyes. There shall be an end to death and pain, for the old order has passed away!'

The throne of God and of the Lamb will be there, and his servants shall worship him; they shall see him face to face and bear his name on their foreheads. There shall be no more night, nor will they need the light of lamp or sun, for the Lord God will give them light; and they shall reign for ever.

Revelation 21.1–4; 22.3b–5

Prayer

Thank you, God,
for the good prospect of heaven,
inhabited by those who have died in the flesh
but risen in the body
as Jesus did before them.
Let me remember them with you,
those I loved here but see no longer,
who now serve and sit with you.
Tell them I love them,
and, if it be your will,
may they be among the first
to welcome me into heaven.

For all the saints who've shown your love

While saints in some cultures refer to the great and the good who have been canonized, there is an equally respectable tradition of using that name for all who have loved God here and have been received into heaven. **An important part of bereavement is to move through grief to gratitude for lives that have touched us and will touch us again.**

FOR ALL THE SAINTS WHO'VE SHOWN YOUR LOVE

WORDS: **John L. Bell**

TUNE: **O waly waly (English traditional), arr. JLB**

For all the saints who've shown your love
in how they live and where they move,
for mindful women, caring men,
accept our gratitude again.

For all the saints who've loved your name,
whose faith increased the Saviour's fame,
who sang your songs and shared your word,
accept our gratitude, good Lord.

For all the saints who named your will,
and show the kingdom coming still
through selfless protest, prayer and praise,
accept the gratitude we raise.

Bless all whose will or name or love
reflects the grace of heaven above.
Though unacclaimed by earthly powers,
your life through theirs has hallowed ours.

In Zion

This magnificent spiritual comes from Tanzania. Like its African-American counterparts, it does not whimper apologetically about a vague nirvana above the bright blue sky, but proclaims proudly that **heaven is a place of song, welcome and reconciliation.**

IN ZION

WORDS: **Jonathan Chambile and F. de Zwart,**
English text by Howard S. Olson
TUNE: **Lupembe, arr. JLB**

In Zion, Lord, with you we'll abide.
Heaven is our home, though untried.
No more doubt; we must decide.
Hear the Saviour calling us; he wants us by his side.
Hear the Saviour calling us; he wants us by his side.

While still here there is work to be done.
The good news to share with each one.
Day departs with setting sun.
It is urgent that all know the great gift, God's own Son.
It is urgent that all know the great gift, God's own Son.

Be ready and await that great day.
When we meet the Lord in dawn's ray.
Purest joy without dismay.
The warm welcome in heaven: it's for this that we pray.
The warm welcome in heaven: it's for this that we pray.

Behold them, countless hosts dressed in white.
Songs are on their lips in the height.
Boundless throngs praising his might.
From each nation all ages praise the Lamb: what a sight.
From each nation all ages praise the Lamb: what a sight.

this song is
DEDICATED
to the people of
DUNBLANE,
AND IN PARTICULAR
TO THE RELATIVES
of the sixteen
PRIMARY SCHOOL

CHILDREN
and their
TEACHER
WHO LOST THEIR
lives
AT THE HAND OF
A GUNMAN ON
13 MARCH 1996

THERE IS A PLACE

WORDS: **John L. Bell & Graham Maule**
TUNE: **Dunblane Primary (JLB)**

There is a place prepared for little children,
those we once lived for, those we deeply mourn,
those who from play, from learning, and from laughter
cruelly were torn.

There is a place where hands which held ours tightly
now are released beyond all hurt and fear,
healed by that love which also feels our sorrow
tear after tear.

There is a place where all the lost potential
yields its full promise, finds its true intent;
silenced no more, young voices echo freely
as they were meant.

There is a place where God will hear our question,
suffer our anger, share our speechless grief,
gently repair the innocence of loving
and of belief.

Jesus, who bids us be like little children,
shields those our arms are yearning to embrace.
God will ensure that all are reunited:
there is a place.

VI. IN THE END

Scripture

There are many dwelling-places in my Father's house; if it were not so I should have told you; for I am going there to prepare a place for you. And if I go and prepare a place for you, I shall come again and take you to myself, so that where I am you may be also.

John 14.2–3

Prayer

I will do it only once, Lord,
though my whole life moves towards it.
So I pray for a good death
when the time is right,
when I have finished my business,
when I have come to terms with my mortality.

Before then,
in the small and large losses of life,
in the giving away of fond possessions,
in the parting of close friends,
in the changing of job, house or church,
may I sense a meaning in loss
and have a foretaste of resurrection.

Aaronic Blessing

The words of the Blessing were first spoken by Moses to Aaron and his sons, as recorded in Numbers 6.24.

AARONIC BLESSING

WORDS: **Traditional**

TUNE: **John L. Bell**

The Lord bless you and keep you.
The Lord make his face to shine upon you
and be gracious unto you.
The Lord lift up his countenance upon you
and give you peace.

Nobody knows

The collection began with a song of the solidarity of Jesus in our grief, and it ends similarly. One of the amazing potentials of the spiritual tradition is how the minimum words can convey both dismay and trust. The situation in which it is sung indicates which condition is being reflected.

NOBODY KNOWS

WORDS: **Traditional**

TUNE: **Traditional, arr. JLB**

Nobody knows the trouble I've seen.
Nobody knows but Jesus.
Nobody knows the trouble I've seen.
Glory, hallelujah!

Sometimes I'm up, sometimes I'm down, oh yes, Lord;
sometimes I'm almost to the ground, oh yes, Lord.

If you get to heaven befo' I do, oh yes, Lord,
tell all my friends I'm comin' too, oh yes, Lord.

Acknowledgements

I am indebted in the first instance to those who have shared both their grief and mine, enabling the text of the original songs to develop. Thereafter, Christine Reid, David McLachlan and Bernard and Sally-Anne Porter helped me with the selection process, offering good advice on pastoral as well as literary and musical issues.

It was a joy, as ever, to work with The Cathedral Singers of Chicago, for whose music and company I have the utmost enthusiasm. And in this I acknowledge that I reap the benefit of what Richard Proulx, their founder and conductor, has sown. Not only did he prepare the choir, but on the first evening of recording, when a storm compelled me to remain for eight hours at Detroit airport, he conducted the session in my stead.

An added and treasured bonus was the presence and participation of Pamela Warrick-Smith, the integrity, beauty and versatility of whose singing deserves wide recognition.

To these artists, as to the five instrumentalists, I offer my congratulations and thanks, as also to Ron Ubel, the engineer who with C. Carroll Cole ensured a disciplined, sensitive and high-quality recording.

Finally, I record my gratitude and that of my colleagues in Scotland to GIA, who commissioned and published this recording, and who have been fond and diligent representatives of our music in North America.

JOHN L. BELL

THE CD

THE CATHEDRAL SINGERS

Soprano: Laura Amend;
Toni Callahan; Lorelei McDermott;
Mary Theresa Reed

Alto: Valerie Glowinski; Alice Kirwan;
Kristi McGonagle; Laura Merkel

Tenor: John Eskola; Paul Huizenga;
Cary Lovett; Frank Villella

Bass: William Chin; William Griffel;
William Haurahan; Tom Orf

THE INSTRUMENTALISTS

Flute: Mary Hickey; *Oboe:* Robert
Morgan; *Cello:* Elizabeth Anderson;
Piano: Kelly Dobbs Mickus; *Organ:*
1922 Ernest M. Skinner, Opus 327

GUEST CONDUCTOR

John L. Bell

EXECUTIVE PRODUCER

Richard Proulx

PRODUCER

C. Carroll Cole

NOTES

John L. Bell

*Recorded in the parish church of Saint Luke,
Evanston, Illinois on 12, 13 and 14 April
1996.*

RECORDING ENGINEERS

Ronald Ubel, Grant Schainost

EDITING ENGINEER

Craig Rettmer

Digital editing and premastering of the compact
disc were completed entirely in the digital
domain using LEXICON'S 'OPUS' Digital
Audio Production System at Soundtrek Studios
in Kansas City, Missouri.